Everything
You Need to
Know About

Cancer

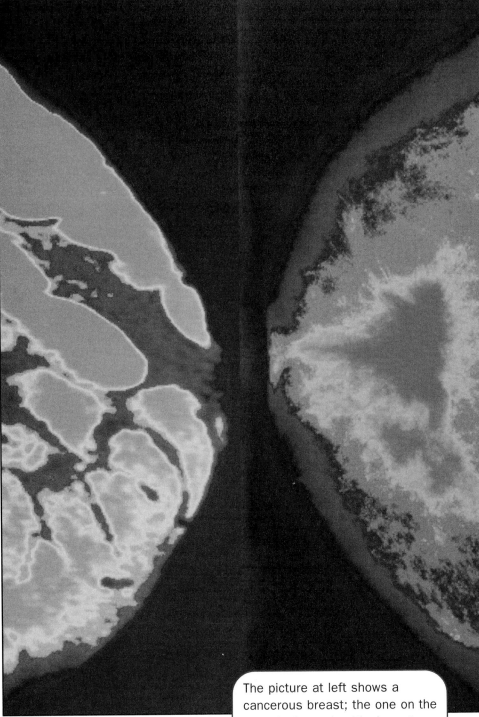

The picture at left shows a cancerous breast; the one on the right depicts a healthy breast.

Everything You Need to Know About Cancer

Francesca Massari

The Rosen Publishing Group, Inc. New York

Published in 2000 by The Rosen Publishing Group, Inc.
29 East 21st Street, New York, NY 10010

First Edition

Library of Congress Cataloging-in-Publication Data

Massari, Francesca.
   Everything you need to know about cancer / Francesca Massari.
      p. cm. — (The need to know library)
   Includes bibliographical references and index.
   Summary: Discusses the nature, causes, prevention, symptoms, diagnosis, and treatment of cancer and provides advice on how to deal with its physical complications and emotional stress.
   ISBN 0-8239-3164-1
   1. Cancer Juvenile literature. [1. Cancer. 2. Diseases.] I. Title. II. Series.
RC264.M47 1999
616.99'4—dc21   99-39647
                                                      CIP
                                                      AC

Manufactured in the United States of America

Contents

Cancer can cause a person to become physically less strong.

Introduction

Hanna was worried about her father. He had trouble playing basketball with Hanna because he was always breathless and coughing. Sometimes he took a break—not to catch his breath, but to smoke a cigarette.

Over time, Hanna noticed that her father's health seemed to be getting a lot worse. He was coughing persistently, sometimes even coughing up blood. Hanna and her mother were so worried that they convinced him to go to the doctor for a checkup. Hanna's mother always said it was important to get an exam as soon as the body gave signs that something was wrong.

The doctor examined Hanna's father and ordered some tests. A few weeks later, Hanna found out that her father had cancer. Years of smoking cigarettes had damaged the cells in her father's lungs. These damaged cells grew into a tumor, resulting in cancer.

Hanna was so upset that she couldn't concentrate in school. This mysterious and horrible thing called cancer was all she thought about. It was making her feel hopeless and angry. She had so many questions but didn't want to upset or bother her parents with them. Finally her teacher, after noticing something was wrong, asked to speak with Hanna after class.

Hanna didn't feel like talking to her teacher about her problem . . . but when Hanna finally opened up, her teacher knew exactly what she was going through. That's because Hanna's teacher had once had cancer herself. She told Hanna about the pain and uncertainty she had experienced. She also told her how important it was to have hope of recovery.

After discussing Hanna's fears, they went to the library to address some of her questions. Hanna learned all about cancer—what causes the disease, what it does to the body, and how to treat it. Hanna also learned about all the support groups that exist to help people like her and her family.

Hanna went home feeling a lot better. She was able to talk to her parents about her father's cancer and her fears. She knew that her father *could die from this disease. But there was also a good chance he would survive. As her teacher had told her, "Today, there are many more people living with cancer than dying from it."*

If you or someone you know has cancer, you are not alone. Half of all men and one-third of all women in the United States will develop cancer at some point in their lives. Right now millions of people are living with cancer. The good news is that the rate of cure has improved in the past few years. Some forms of cancer can be cured with chemotherapy alone or with a combination of treatments. Many cancer patients who cannot be fully cured are nonetheless living longer and fuller lives than they would have in the past.

A diagnosis of cancer, whether in yourself or in a friend or family member, is a very difficult thing to deal with. Your first reaction may be disbelief, fear, confusion, anger, helplessness, or all of these. Understanding cancer is the first step in dealing with this major life challenge.

In this book, you will learn what cancer is and what causes it. You will learn about the symptoms and treatments of different cancers. You will learn about the support systems that are available to help you deal with it successfully. Most important, you will learn that people have survived all types of cancer.

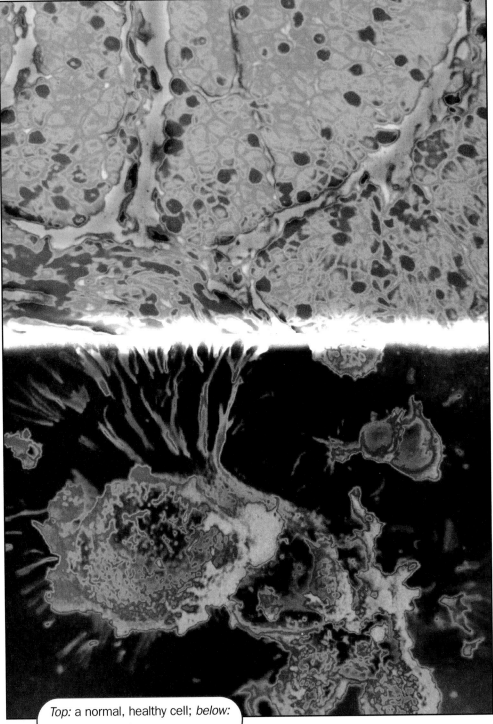

Top: a normal, healthy cell; *below:* a cell that has become cancerous.

Chapter One

What Is Cancer?

Cancer is not really one disease but a group of over 200 related diseases. Cancer is the result of some cells in the body reproducing uncontrollably. These cells pile up on each other and may spread to other parts of the body. As these cells invade organs in the body, they have the potential to damage or destroy them.

How Does Cancer Start?

The normal cells in our bodies have genetic instructions inside of them telling them when to multiply, when to reproduce, and when to die. Cancer begins when a cell mutates and multiplies in an uncontrollable way. This may be caused by a genetic flaw, exposure to cancer-causing agents, radiation, viruses, or other unknown causes.

Primary Tumors

Usually cancer starts growing in one place. This is called the primary site. As the cancer cells multiply, they pile up on each other and form a lump called a tumor. The tumor that forms at the primary site is called a primary tumor.

Cancer cells can keep multiplying until they reach and invade a neighboring area. They do this by crossing the boundary that separates one group of normal cells from the next. Most normal cells cannot cross this boundary, which is called a basement membrane. However, cancer cells produce certain substances that allow them to break through this membrane.

Are All Tumors Bad?

There are two types of tumors: benign and malignant. A benign tumor is not cancerous. It poses no threat to a body's health because it stops growing. A malignant tumor is cancerous. A malignant tumor continues to grow and to invade neighboring areas.

Secondary Tumors

If cancers were able to invade only these neighboring areas, they would be curable in most cases. A doctor would be able to locate the tumor, check the surrounding areas, and remove the cancerous cells by surgery. Unfortunately, this is not the case. What makes cancer so dangerous is that cancer cells can move to other, more distant parts of the body. This process is called metastasis.

When cancer metastasizes, or spreads, cancer cells can be lodged in different organs in the body. Cancer cells spread this way by breaking away from the primary tumor and getting into the bloodstream or lymph nodes. It's like catching a train. Cancer cells move into the bloodstream or the lymph nodes and can travel to any place in the body.

Once these cancer cells exit the bloodstream or lymph nodes, they house themselves in an organ and grow new malignant tumors, called secondary tumors. As these tumors grow, they can disrupt or destroy the proper function of the organ they have invaded.

Cancer cells can do all of the following:

- Continue to grow and multiply
- Invade surrounding areas
- Spread to other parts of the body, moving through the bloodstream or the lymph nodes
- Create secondary tumors, or metastasize in these distant areas
- Produce substances that negatively affect bodily functions or parts of the body

Why Are Some Cancers More Harmful Than Others?

Some cancers are potentially serious, and others are rarely life threatening. Each type of cancer has its own way of behaving. Although some cancers have a high tendency to spread to other parts of the body, many others do not. This means that different cancers vary in their potential to cause harm. The cancers that spread to other parts of the body are the most harmful.

Classifying Cancer

Although cancer may spread to different places in your body, cancer is classified by where the cancer started. So if a cancer started in the stomach and spread to the liver, it would be classified as stomach cancer and not liver cancer.

How Do Tumors Live?

When something foreign enters our bodies, certain cells have an immune reaction and fight it off. However, because cancer cells are normal cells gone wrong, there is no immune reaction against them. Tumors easily establish their own territory. Cancer cells also trick nearby tissues to form new blood vessels to bring the cancer cells their own blood supply. This blood supply nourishes the cancer cells and allows them to keep growing.

Is Cancer More Common Now Than Ever?

Cancer has been around probably as long as humans have. In earlier times, diseases such as tuberculosis, cholera, smallpox, and the bubonic plague were much more threatening and harmful than cancer. Now that we have found cures for these other diseases, cancer seems more terrible to us. Also, people are living longer today. In earlier times, people died before reaching the age when cancer usually appears (the late 50s and older). More people have cancer now than in the past, not because cancer is on the rise, but because more people are living long enough to develop it.

Chapter Two

What Causes Cancer?

Jon's family has a history of cancer. His grandfather, two uncles, and a cousin all had cancer at some point in their lives. When Jon's mom got breast cancer, he wanted to know what caused it. Was cancer something that was inherited? What did it mean if cancer ran in families? Would he get cancer someday too, or could he actively work to prevent it?

When Sasha got cancer, it was a huge shock to the whole family. None of Sasha's relatives had had cancer, but three people in her neighborhood had been diagnosed with cancer in recent months. Could there be something in the environment that was causing Sasha and her neighbors to become ill? Could something in the environment, some toxic chemical, cause cancer?

The truth is that we do not know all the causes of cancer. For some cancers, such as brain cancer and Hodgkin's disease, we have very few clues as to what causes them. For other cancers, such as breast and lung cancer, although we do not know what causes them, we do know what factors make them likely to develop.

Most cancers are caused by a combination of factors. The two main factors are genes and the environment. Each gene in the body—with the exception of certain genes in the reproductive system—contains twenty-three pairs of chromosomes, on which all the body's genetic information is contained. In certain cases, for reasons that are not completely understood, genes go haywire, reproduce out of control, and become cancerous.

Usually this genetic tendency alone is not strong enough to cause cancer. This tendency can be thought of as a susceptibility or vulnerability to cancer-causing agents. Such agents are known as carcinogens. Most types of cancer emerge only after the vulnerability of such cells is triggered by contact with unhealthy things in the environment. Environmental triggers include exposure to toxic chemicals, radiation, a high-fat diet, excessive sunlight, and tobacco.

Damage to the Genetic Material

Virtually any cell in a person's body can become cancerous. Scientists now believe that what makes a cell

Smoking is one of the leading causes of cancer.

become cancerous is damage to its DNA, the genetic material inside the nucleus of the cell. Certain chemicals, such as acid, can destroy cells but not their DNA. These chemicals will not cause cancer. Other chemicals, such as some of those found in cigarettes, damage the genetic material of cells. The damage done to these cells stays with the person forever.

Over time, as cells suffer greater exposure to carcinogens, the damage adds up, causing a greater chance that cancer will develop. That's why long-term exposure to a carcinogen, such as years of sitting in the sun or smoking, is so harmful.

How Much Damage Can a Cell's DNA Take?

The amount of a toxin a normal cell can handle without

becoming cancerous will vary from person to person and cell to cell. Normal cells in the body have different tendencies toward becoming cancerous. Some cells are highly resistant to becoming malignant or diseased. These cells can withstand a lot of damage from environmental triggers. Other cells seem to be always on the edge of becoming cancerous. They would require less radiation, tobacco smoke, sunlight (ultraviolet rays), or other factors to trigger a cancerous reaction.

Tumor-Suppressor Genes

Scientists believe that some cells are designed to become cancerous all on their own. What stops them from becoming cancerous are genes called tumor-suppressor genes. The tumor-suppressor genes actually stop cells from abnormal and out-of-control growth. It is only when these tumor-suppressor genes are lost or destroyed that the cells are able to become cancerous.

The Oncogene

One type of gene that seems to be involved in several cancers is called an oncogene. Oncogenes are genes that control a few normal functions of the cell but change their behavior when exposed to cancer-causing agents. The oncogenes appear to help normal cells become cancerous. Oncogenes are not necessarily involved in all cancers, however. Some cells can become cancerous without the help of the oncogene.

Environmental Triggers and Risk Factors

To some degree, everyone is exposed to potential carcinogens, such as cigarettes, radiation, gasoline, pesticides, sunlight, viruses, and bacteria. Exposure to any one of these is called a risk factor. A risk factor increases one's chance of getting cancer. Smoking cigarettes, for example, is a risk factor for cancer of the lungs, mouth, throat, bladder, and larynx.

The longer a person is exposed to these harmful agents, the higher the risk of developing cancer. However, just because a person has a risk factor does not mean that he or she will develop cancer. Likewise, the fact that someone has no known risk factors does not mean that this person will never develop cancer.

If cancer runs in your family, that is another risk factor. Some cancers occur with greater frequency among relatives. Breast, ovarian, and colon cancer occur at higher rates than normal among relatives. If a woman's sibling or mother has breast cancer, her risk of developing breast cancer herself doubles. That makes it all the more important for her to stay away from environmental carcinogens. A few cancers occur because a flawed gene is passed from parent to child,

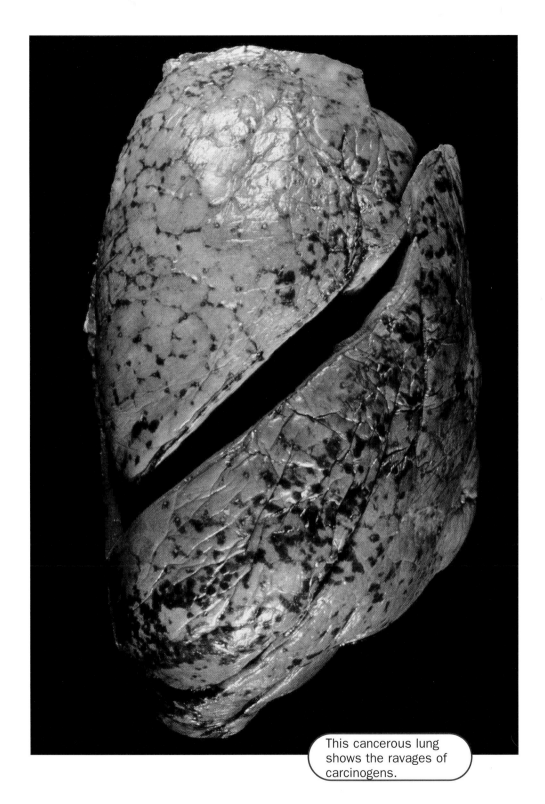

This cancerous lung shows the ravages of carcinogens.

but this is very rare. Some specific risk factors and the specific cancers they cause are given below:

- *High-fat diet/inactivity/obesity*—breast, endometrial, and colon cancers

- *Smoking*—lung, cervical, bladder, lip, mouth, nose, and throat cancers

- *Chewing tobacco*—mouth and lip cancers

- *Asbestos*—lung cancer

- *Sunlight*—melanoma (skin cancer)

- *Radiation*—leukemias

- *Viruses/parasites/bacteria*—liver, cervical, bladder, and colon cancers

Chapter Three

Can Cancer Be Prevented?

Kelly had always loved the way her skin looked at the peak of summer. She had sunbathed at the hottest time of the day so that she could achieve a dark bronze tan as fast as possible. Her mother had always told her to use sunscreen, but Kelly didn't listen. She just couldn't believe it would make any difference in her life. Years later, Kelly noticed that a mole on her stomach had changed size and shape. Fortunately she knew enough to consult a doctor right away. The diagnosis was what her mother had always warned her about— melanoma, or skin cancer. Luckily, early detection made Kelly's prognosis good, but she was still upset with herself because she knew that she could have done more to prevent the disease. She vowed

Using sunscreen can decrease your risk for skin cancer.

that her own children, when she had them, would not make the same mistake.

Risk Factors

For many types of cancer, there are steps you can take toward prevention. Prevention means avoiding or minimizing risk factors in order to reduce the likelihood of getting cancer. Knowing what those risk factors are is the first step in prevention.

Prevention is not always easy. At times, it may mean giving up things that you enjoy, such as smoking, sunbathing, or eating and drinking certain kinds of food. It may mean making decisions based not on the pleasure of the moment but on your future health.

Sun Exposure

Each year in the United States, there are approximately 600,000 new cases of melanoma, or skin cancer. Many of them could be prevented if people protected themselves from the sun's damaging rays. It is common knowledge now that wearing sunscreen will help prevent skin cancer, but many people still refuse to wear it. As a preventive measure, people should avoid suntanning during the peak harmful hours between 11 AM and 3 PM, wear sunblock (at least SPF 15), wear a hat if possible, and avoid getting sunburned. If you've had three blistering sunburns before age twenty, your risk of getting melanoma may be increased fivefold. Despite the knowledge we now have about how to prevent skin cancer, its incidence is still rising at a rate of 4 percent each year.

Tobacco and Alcohol Use

Experts estimate that at least 85 percent of lung cancer deaths and 30 percent of all cancer deaths are caused by tobacco use. If people stopped smoking and chewing tobacco, 175,000 cancer deaths each year would be prevented. If everyone in the United States gave up smoking right this minute, the lung cancer rate three decades from now would be reduced an estimated 90 percent. Heavy drinking—defined as the equivalent of more than one drink each day—leads to 19,000 fatal cases of cancer each year in the United States. Heavy drinking is

Heavy drinking contributes to various forms of cancer.

most often implicated in cancer of the liver, stomach, or pancreas. Obviously, heavy drinking is another risk factor that is within each individual's control.

Smokers: The Sooner You Quit, the Better

A recent study showed that the cancer patients with the worst genetic damage to their lungs were those who started smoking at the youngest age, not those who have been smoking the longest. Scientists speculate that lungs that are not yet fully developed, like those of young people, are more susceptible to the kind of long-term damage that leads to cancer. That means that young smokers may be at high risk for developing cancer. So don't take the risk. Quit now. And if you haven't started, that's even better. Don't!

Diet

According to scientists, one-third of all cancer deaths this year in the United States are related to poor nutrition—both overnutrition and undernutrition. A diet high in fat (over 25 percent of total daily calories) has been linked to cancer. Some researchers believe that as fat is digested, it produces cancer-causing chemicals. A diet low in fiber has also been linked to colon cancer. It is believed that fiber helps move cancer-causing agents through the colon faster. Without fiber, the foods containing carcinogens linger in the colon and negatively affect it.

Taking care of your body through proper diet is another preventative measure that is well within your control. It is up to you to take care of your body and work hard to keep it healthy. The American Cancer Society recommends these cancer prevention guidelines:

- Eat vegetables, fruit, and whole grains every day.
- Reduce fat intake to less than 25 percent of total daily calories.
- Maintain a healthy weight.
- Exercise.
- Limit the amount of the following salt-cured, smoked, and nitrate-cured foods: sausage, bacon, lunch meats, hot dogs, fried meat, and fried fish.

High-fiber foods can cut your risk of colon cancer.

Age

Some risk factors linked to cancer cannot be prevented. Age is one such factor. Age is the single most important risk factor for cancer. Over half of all cancers occur in people over sixty-five years old. It makes sense that the more years you are exposed to a harmful cancer-causing agent, the greater the chance that cancer will develop. Because cancer is so common among older people, it is very important for them to get health exams and cancer screenings on a regular basis.

Getting Screened

Screening means performing diagnostic tests on people who have no symptoms. For example, all healthy women who are sexually active should get periodic Pap tests, which are used to detect cancer of the cervix. A rectal exam should be done on all men over the age of forty to test for cancers of the prostate and colon. Other screening tests can be given to people with high risk factors for the development of specific types of cancer. Women who have two or more relatives with breast cancer, for example, should be screened for the presence of certain genes.

Why Is Early Detection So Difficult?

The earlier cancer is detected, the better the chances are for survival. The problem with early screening tests is that they cannot usually detect the potential for developing cancer. Screening tests (except for the Pap test) can only detect the cancer after it has developed.

Why Is Cancer Detected So Late?

When a cancer starts to grow, it is very small. The average human cell is about 1/20th of the width of a piece of hair. Even if there are a million cancer cells clumped together, the mass would be only about the size of a pinhead. So before a tumor can even be detected inside the body, it has to form a billion cells, which would make it the size of a grape. It takes the average cancer cell two and a half years to grow to this size. It would take about three and a half years of growth for that initial cancer cell to grow large enough to be fatal to the human body.

This explains one of the main problems with cancer prevention: By the time a tumor can be detected, it is already well developed and likely to constitute an immediate health hazard. For this reason, once cancer is detected, action must be taken very quickly to fight it.

Chapter Four | What Are the Symptoms of Cancer?

*W*hen Janice felt a lump in her breast, she panicked. Her mother had breast cancer, and Janice knew that some cancers, including breast cancer, occur with greater frequency among relatives.

Janice went to the doctor immediately, which was the right thing to do. The doctor told her that most lumps in the breast are not cancer. Breast cancer often does not cause any specific symptoms. However, any lump should be treated as a warning sign. Sometimes the breast may tingle or the nipple may invert (caused by the tumor pulling on it). Identifying a lump in the breast as cancer requires testing by a doctor.

Janice's doctor did not think the lump felt cancerous. To be sure, he took an X ray of her breast.

It's important to be screened for cancer, especially if it runs in your family.

Such an X ray is called a mammogram. In many cases, breast cancer is detected by routine screening as part of regular health checkups. If the X ray shows a potential tumor, it needs to be examined further, which is usually done by ultrasound testing. An ultrasound will show whether the tumor is a solid lump or a cyst.

A cyst is filled with fluid and is not cancerous. If a solid lump is found, the doctor will order a biopsy. A biopsy is the surgical removal of a piece of the lump for closer examination in a laboratory. This will show if the lump is cancerous or benign. For young women, chances are the lump will be benign.

One morning when Molly got out of the shower, she noticed that a mole on her neck seemed to have changed color. She was sure it had always been brown, but now it was black with purple and brown areas in it. It looked larger than usual and there were smaller moles growing around it. Molly showed her mother, who was a nurse. Her mother knew these were the classic symptoms of melanoma. They made an appointment to see Molly's doctor, who confirmed their suspicions and diagnosed Molly with melanoma. The good news is that the doctor was able to perform surgery on Molly's moles and to remove all of the cancer. Today Molly is cancer-free because she noticed a change in her body and took action to have a doctor look at it.

Symptoms of Cancer

Pain, fatigue, and depression are the most common symptoms experienced by people with cancer. However, cancer can cause almost any type of symptom, and many of the symptoms caused by cancer are also caused by much less serious conditions.

Headaches, for example, are far more likely to be due to stress than to brain cancer. Pain in the stomach is more likely to be due to an ulcer or indigestion than to stomach cancer. Although extreme tiredness, lumps, or sudden weight loss are symptoms of cancer, it is also much more likely they are caused by a less serious disease. You cannot assume you have cancer just because you have a symptom of cancer. Certainly, any one of these symptoms, if it occurs with any frequency or severity, is a good reason to consult a doctor.

The only way to be sure if you have cancer is to see a doctor and to be tested. Most people with cancer do not start off experiencing any pain, which is one reason cancer is so hard to detect in its early stages. Pain, however, does occur in almost two-thirds of all patients with advanced cancer.

Pain does not come from the tumor itself. Pain occurs when the tumor presses on or interferes with certain organs, tissues, or nerves in the body. The good news is that the pain can be stopped or lessened in nine out of ten patients with the right medication.

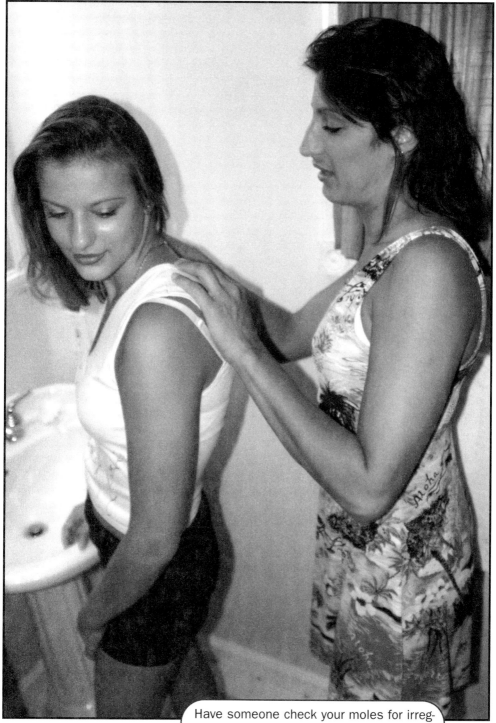

Have someone check your moles for irreg-
ularities and changes in size or shape.

Find out about your family's history of cancer.

What to Do If You Think You Have Cancer

If you find a lump or you think that your body is behaving strangely, make an appointment to see your doctor. Write down the symptoms you are experiencing and try to describe any pain you may have as clearly as you can. Ask your parents or other family members about your family's history of cancer. The doctor will want to know what specific types of cancer run in your family.

Chapter Five

The Diagnosis and Treatment of Cancer

*J*ack felt what he thought was a pimple in his left armpit. He kept rubbing it and waiting for it to go away, but it didn't. It grew bigger—almost an inch around. It didn't hurt, so he didn't think it was harmful, just irritating. It was Jack's girlfriend who told him that the growth was no pimple—it was a lump! She sent him straight to the doctor for an exam.

The doctor told Jack that he had an enlarged lymph node. Usually swollen lymph nodes are caused by common, everyday infections. However, these usually appear when a person is sick and disappear in a few weeks. Jack had no other symptoms. His doctor thought the enlarged lymph node looked suspicious, so he ordered a test called a biopsy.

Jack didn't know what a biopsy was. He was the type of guy who hated to have his blood drawn. He told the doctor he felt fine and didn't need any tests. The doctor explained that a biopsy was necessary to see if the cells that were forming the lump were cancerous or not. A biopsy is the removal of cells so they can be examined under a microscope for signs of cancer.

Jack was given a local anesthetic, and a doctor removed a piece of the lymph node from his armpit. The piece was then sent to the lab to be examined. Jack went home and waited for the results. His girlfriend told him everything would be okay, and Jack tried not to worry.

A week later, Jack's doctor called him and said that they needed to speak. He told his parents, and they accompanied him to the doctor's office. The doctor told them that his biopsy showed a malignancy. Jack had cancer.

"Cancer?" Jack asked. "You've got to be kidding."

"My son can't have cancer," Jack's mom said. "He's young and healthy."

"I'm sorry," the doctor said. "We'll have to run some more tests to see how far it has advanced."

Jack and his parents let the idea wash over them, but they still couldn't accept what they were hearing. They thought the doctor must have made some sort of terrible mistake and mixed up the biopsies of two patients. Jack was young and feeling healthy! How could a young man come to the doctor with a pimple and leave with a diagnosis of cancer?

Jack's family left the hospital feeling lower than they had ever felt. Over the next few weeks, they felt anger, disbelief, fear, depression, and sadness. Jack had other tests done to determine which type of lymphoma (cancer of the lymph nodes) he had and what stage it had reached. Ultimately, Jack was diagnosed with non-Hodgkin's lymphoma.

Surgery was performed to remove the enlarged lymph node, but the surgeon found that the cancer was spreading. Soon, Jack began to feel the symptoms of his disease: tiredness, weight loss, fever, and night sweats. More surgery was needed. Jack had to spend a long time in the hospital, and his family began to pray more than ever for his recovery. They spent a lot of time talking and appreciating the little things of day-to-day life.

After seven months in the hospital, Jack recovered. Although there was no absolute guarantee the disease would not ever resurface, in medical terms Jack was cured. This ordeal was over. The disease had lost. He and his family could go home and spread the wonderful news of recovery.

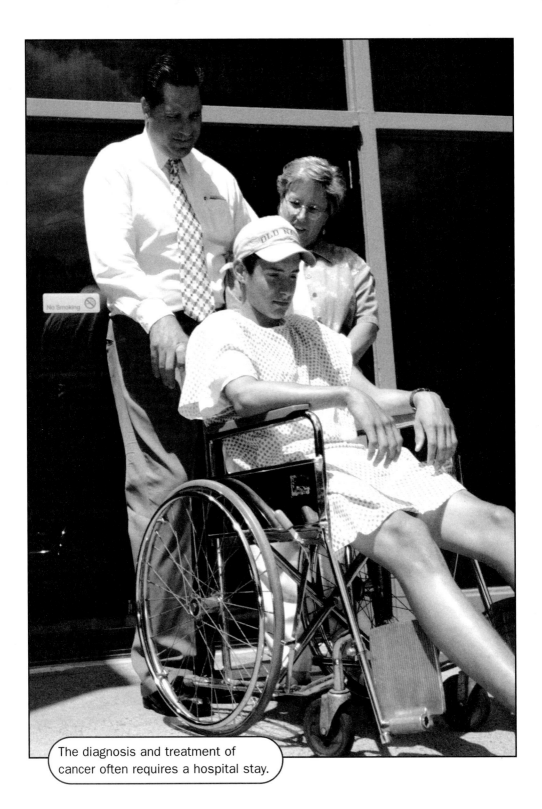

The diagnosis and treatment of cancer often requires a hospital stay.

Clinical History and Physical Examination

When you first visit your doctor, he or she will want to know if your parents, grandparents, or siblings have had cancer. If so, the doctor will need to know what type of cancer it was. This is called taking a family history. If the doctor has not treated you before, he or she will also ask you a lot of questions about your past medical history, illnesses you may have had, and your exposure to various risk factors.

The doctor will examine your overall physical health and then address your symptom or symptoms. If you are worried about a lump, for example, your doctor may know immediately if the lump is a harmless fatty deposit or something more serious. If the doctor is unsure, he or she will probably order some more tests. This is routine and is not necessarily a reason for any more worry.

Biopsy

Sometimes the doctor will need to send cells from the tumor or lump to a laboratory to be examined under a microscope. To do this, the physician removes a piece of tissue (using a very simple and fast surgery) from the lump. This is called a biopsy.

By examining the tumor cells under the microscope, the doctor can determine what kind of cells they are. Normal cells are all the same size and grow in orderly rows. Cancer cells are different sizes and are heaped all over each other. The nucleus of each cancer cell is much larger than that in a normal cell. From the biopsy, the doctor will be able to tell not only whether the growth is cancerous but what kind of cancer it is.

Blood Tests

Blood tests can be used to reveal where the cancer exists in the body. The most commonly used type of blood test is called a marker. A marker can show if a certain type of protein in the blood is at an abnormally high level. For example, a high level of the protein called PSA (prostate-specific antigen) means that the patient may have prostate cancer. A high level of the protein called CEA (carcino-embryonic antigen) means the patient may have bowel or breast cancer.

Scans and X Rays

Different exams are used to test for different types of cancer. If there is a possibility of lung cancer, then an X ray of the chest will be taken. If a lump is found in the neck, a scan of the thyroid may be done. A scan called a mammogram helps to detect cancer of the breast.

A CAT (computerized axial tomography) scan may be used for many different types of cancer. The CAT scan is really an X ray with a computer system that analyzes how the X rays are changed as they pass through the body. CAT scans are used to determine if the cancer has spread to other parts of the body. Using the CAT scan, the doctor can see what stage the cancer has reached.

What Are the Stages of Cancer?

There are four basic stages of cancer. Stage A cancers are microscopic. Stage B cancers are palpable, meaning they are large enough to be felt as a lump or nodule. Stage C cancers have spread from the primary site into surrounding areas. Stage D cancers have metastasized to the lymph nodes or bones and possibly to other tissues as well.

Treatment

The earlier that cancer is detected, the earlier treatment can begin, and the better a patient's chances are for a cure. There are many different types of treatment for curing cancer. The type of treatment used will vary for each person.

Different people respond differently to the same type of treatment. That's because just as we all look a little different on the outside, we all vary a little on the inside. Small changes in our biochemical makeup can alter how our bodies accept or reject certain treatments. Cancer itself works differently in different people,

depending on various factors. There are three important factors in determining which treatment program is
used: the stage of cancer, or whether it has spread to
other parts of the body; the rate of growth of the
tumor; and the grade of the tumor, meaning what it
looks like under the microscope.

Surgery

Surgical removal of the tumor is the oldest type of
medical treatment for cancer. It has been used for about
2,000 years, and the technique has improved tremen-
dously over that time. Some 60 percent of all cancer
patients will have some type of surgery. It offers the
best chance of a cure when the tumor exists in only one
place and has not spread.

Radiotherapy or Radiation Therapy

This treatment was first used to treat cancer in France
about 100 years ago. Radiotherapy is the use of very
powerful X rays that give off a certain type of radiation called gamma rays. These gamma rays can kill the
cells in their path. Radiotherapy is directed at the part
of the body that is overcome with cancer cells. The
major drawback of radiation is that because it cannot
distinguish between healthy and cancerous cells, it dam-
ages or destroys all cells in the area. The result can be
severe side effects, including nausea, difficulty swallow-
ing, diarrhea, fatigue, loss of appetite, and hair loss. Like

surgery, radiation is generally not effective if cancer cells have spread throughout the body from the original tumor.

Chemotherapy

This type of treatment has been used to treat cancer for almost sixty years. Chemotherapy is the use of certain drugs, sometimes in combination, to kill cells that are multiplying very rapidly. The drugs used in chemotherapy are unable to distinguish between cancer cells and normal cells that reproduce rapidly, so both kinds of cells are damaged by chemotherapy. However, cancer cells suffer the most damage. That's because there are usually more cancer cells than normal cells growing at a fast rate.

Certain cells, such as those in the bone marrow, digestive tract, and hair, are always multiplying at a rapid rate. That means that chemotherapy is likely to affect these parts of the body. You may have seen some cancer patients with little or no hair. That is the direct result of some, but not all, chemotherapy drugs. When the chemotherapy treatment ends, the patient's hair will grow back.

Because the drugs affect the bone marrow, which makes white and red blood cells, chemotherapy can reduce the number of white blood cells, or leukocytes, in your body. Because your body's immune system uses white blood cells to fight off infection, any reduction in the number of leukocytes increases your susceptibility to infection. Doctors will therefore sometimes prescribe

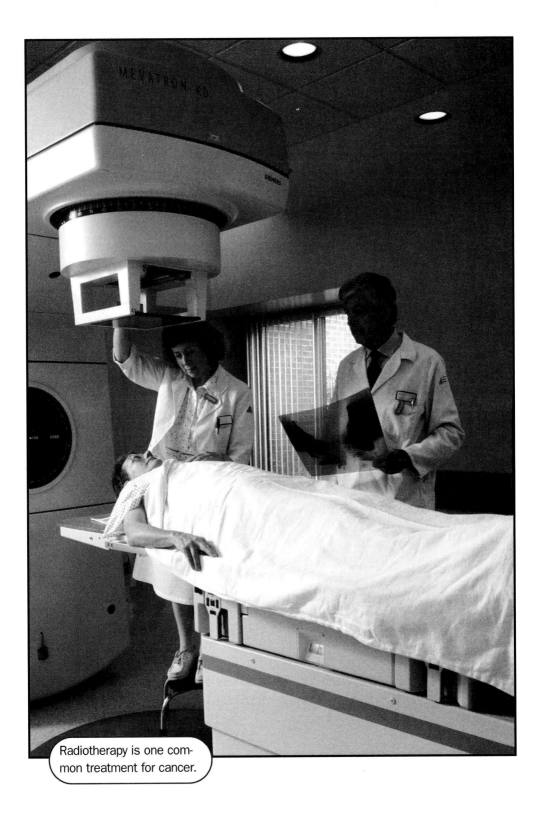

Radiotherapy is one common treatment for cancer.

antibiotics for chemotherapy patients to help them fight off infection. Chemotherapy drugs are injected into a vein or are taken orally. These drugs use the bloodstream to reach all parts of the body. This way, if the cancer cells have spread throughout the body, the drugs can reach them and destroy them.

Side Effects of Chemotherapy

Almost all chemotherapy drugs cause some side effects. The most common side effects are nausea, vomiting, and fatigue. Nausea usually begins a few hours after treatment and may continue for a day or so. There are drugs called antinauseants that may help to control the nausea. Fatigue may linger until a month after treatment ends.

Different chemotherapy drugs can cause different side effects, including loss of appetite, numbness or tingling in the toes, a metallic taste to food, diarrhea, and buzzing in the ears. Most normal cells recover quickly once chemotherapy treatment ends, so most side effects gradually disappear at the end of treatment. Other side effects, however, may take months or years to disappear. It is also possible that certain side effects can last a lifetime; in particular the lungs, kidneys, heart, or reproductive organs can suffer permanent damage. Be sure to ask your doctor what the known side effects are for the chemotherapy drugs he or she has prescribed.

Although the side effects of chemotherapy are unpleasant, the benefits of chemotherapy far outweigh the problems it causes. Chemotherapy can cure cancer, keep the cancer from spreading, relieve symptoms that may be caused by cancer, and help people live more comfortably.

Biologic Therapy or Immunotherapy

Biologic therapy has been used for only about ten years and is not very advanced at this time. The goal of this type of therapy is to change certain aspects of the immune system in order to make it more effective in fighting cancer. For example, biologic therapy uses antibodies to carry toxins or chemotherapy drugs directly to the site of the cancer. That way, normal, healthy cells will not be affected by the drugs.

Combining Treatments

Most cancer patients today receive a combination of treatments. This means that most cancer patients will be seen and treated by several different doctors and health care technicians, including their primary care physician, a surgeon (who operates), a radiologist (who administers radiotherapy), and an oncologist (a specialist in tumors who prescribes drugs or administers chemotherapy). Just because you need to see different types of doctors does not mean you have an especially bad case of cancer.

Does Treatment Work?

About half of the total amount of cancer patients will be cured with treatment. Most of these cures are due to surgery. Radiotherapy (with or without surgery) and chemotherapy lead to the other cures. Even when a cure is not possible, these treatments may lead to remission, which is a lessening of symptoms for a period of time. Every person with cancer has the right to a comprehensive and realistic discussion with his or her doctor(s) about the chance of a successful treatment.

Remission Versus Cure

A cure means that over a continuous specified period of time—usually five years—there is no evidence of cancer in the body. At that point, physicians speak of a cure, although there is no absolute guarantee that the cancer will not ever return. Sometimes there can be no evidence of cancer in a person for a period of time, but the cancer still returns. This is called a recurrence and can happen if cancer cells are able to hide away in some part of the body without being detected. Some cancers may recur up to twenty years later.

A remission means that the cancer has become smaller and the symptoms have eased or lessened. Even with the most successful treatment, it is impossible to know whether all the cancer cells have been destroyed. That is why a recurrence is possible even in a patient who has been "cured." The likelihood that a recurrence will take place depends of the type of cancer.

Chapter Six

Living with Cancer: Giving and Getting Help

When Anna was first told she had cancer, her body felt numb and her mind went blank. It seemed like a horrendously bad dream. Anna's family tried comforting her, but she wouldn't let them. They tried talking about it, but she wouldn't listen. She locked herself in her bedroom and cried. She felt so alone and angry. She was sure her best friends wouldn't understand what she was going through, and the last thing she wanted was their pity. Her friends tried calling her, but she refused to answer the phone. Finally, they stopped calling her altogether. After another week of misery, Anna picked up the phone and called her friends. Rather than finding pity, she found solace. The more Anna opened up to her friends, the better she felt.

Eventually, Anna realized that emotional support was just as important as medical treatment.

Her parents suggested that she join a special cancer support group for teens. They thought Anna would benefit from being around other young people who were also fighting cancer. It turned out that they were right. The support group gave Anna a way to express her emotions. She learned that she was not in this fight alone.

What You May Feel

Physical symptoms are one thing, but what do people feel emotionally when they learn that they have cancer? Most people feel shock, anger, fear, guilt, and awkwardness. Some feel humiliated or embarrassed. Finding out that your life is threatened by a disease is as great an emotional trauma as you can experience. Thinking about all that lies ahead of you can be truly overwhelming.

At first, many people try to block out the news by denying it altogether. Denial can be a very complicated process. Denial does not necessarily mean convincing yourself that in fact you don't really have cancer. Instead, it is a process of avoiding or ignoring the complicated emotional responses that arise from a realistic assessment of the consequences of your diagnosis. Denial is a quite normal emotional response that gives you time to take in the news slowly and then accept it.

Some people even feel as though they did something wrong to bring cancer upon themselves. Other people may not be used to talking about sensitive matters and sharing intimate feelings. You may be afraid of how others will react or how you and your family will deal with it all. No matter what your feelings are, there are ways to help you deal with them. Most of the time, this will involve talking about your feelings to the right person. That doesn't mean your feelings need to be changed. If you feel that you do want to talk things over, be prepared to ask lots of questions.

Telling Family and Friends

When you tell somebody close to you that you have cancer, the person may experience some of what you yourself feel, such as shock or sadness. Sometimes it is harder to deal with the emotions of your family or friends than with your own. Your friends might panic because they want to make you feel better and say the right thing, but they may not know what the right thing to say is. In truth, there is no right or wrong thing to say.

You may even feel like you have to pretend everything is okay to make everyone feel better. Help them to relax by being as honest as possible. It may be painful or awkward for both you and your friends at first, but as time passes and they come to accept that you have cancer, things will improve. They will see that you are still the same person you were before the diagnosis, with the same interests and ability to have fun.

Ask for Information

Doctors are there to help you. If you do not understand any medical terms, ask your doctor or nurse to explain them. It's a good idea to take family or friends along with you for a question and answer session to help you remember everything that was said. You can also check out library books or visit Web sites to get information. Knowing about your disease and what to expect will make you feel much more in control of your life.

Getting Support

There are lots of people you can turn to for help. School counselors, clergy, doctors, nurses, friends, family, and support groups are all available to you. Often family and friends are the best people to comfort and reassure you. Other times, you may feel that they just don't get whatever it is you're going through. That's when a support group becomes so important. With a support group, you can talk to people about your pain or fear and they can tell you how they got through their toughest moments.

Scientific studies show that being an active member of a support group can actually lengthen a cancer patient's life! There are all kinds of support groups available for teens and adults. For information on how to find a support group, see the Where to Go for Help section at the back of this book.

You can find many forms of support on the Web.

Giving Support

It is important to know what a friend with cancer is facing. The fact that your friend has a disease may be difficult for him or her to accept. Uncertainty, or not knowing what will happen, may be the hardest thing for your friend to accept. You can help by telling your friend that you understand this. Your friend may be in a lot of pain or may feel uncomfortable about the side effects of chemotherapy treatment, such as hair loss. The best medicine for this is to show your friend that you care.

If someone you know has cancer, you may feel as though you should say or do certain things to help the person. There is no single correct thing to say or do. You will not have all the answers, so don't pretend that you do.

Instead, you may want to focus on being a good listener. The act of talking out a problem, in itself, makes people feel better. Just by listening to a person, you may help him or her release some stress. All it takes to be a good listener is to listen and think about what the person is saying.

Asking your friend some tough questions can help, too. For example, don't think that you can't ask your friend if he or she is worried about getting chemotherapy. If you think your friend is worried about something, you can encourage your friend to talk about it. Not talking about our fears only makes our fears stronger. Once we talk about them, they lose some of their power.

There are lots of ways to help others with cancer. The most important thing is to tell the person how you feel about him or her. Be a good listener. Know that it's okay to express your fears. Remember to be yourself and act natural. You can still tell jokes—humor can be very healing! Visit the person often. Be hopeful; even if a cure is unlikely, you can be positive about ordinary things in the person's day-to-day life. You can also help out with chores, especially if the patient is your parent.

Grieving

Although many patients are cured of cancer, many others die from the disease. Dying is something that will happen to all of us, yet most people do not like to talk about it, even when it has happened to someone they love. Ignoring it, however, will not make it go away. You may start off by denying that what is happening is real, and that is a perfectly natural response.

After a while, your feelings will change. You may become angry, shocked, or depressed. You may feel scared. This is the process of grief. Talking to friends or family is important at this time. If you don't feel like talking to anybody about it, you may want to keep a journal in which you record your thoughts and your memories of the person who has passed away. You may feel like the pain will never go away, that you will not be able to face life without this person. However, eventually you will find peace with the idea of death and knowing that this person lives on in your memories.

Looking to the Future

Life does not stop with a diagnosis of cancer. Most people can lead happy, productive lives with cancer. For a while things may seem very hard, and you may worry that life will never get back to normal. Just remember that life is full of challenges for everyone and that each challenge eventually ends. How will you face your challenges? Balance the time spent at the hospital with time spent with friends or doing a favorite activity. Think ahead to the time when treatment is over and you are healthy again. Most important, be hopeful about your future and enjoy each day to the fullest.

Glossary

basement membrane A wall or barrier between normal cells that separates one group of normal cells from another. Cancerous cells penetrate this membrane by producing an enzyme that breaks down these walls.

benign Presenting little or no threat to health or life; used to describe a non-cancerous tumor.

biopsy The removal and examination of tissue, cells, or fluids from the living body.

chemotherapy The use of drugs to treat cancer.

cure Recovery or relief from a disease.

immune system The bodily system that protects the body from infection by foreign substances. It includes the thymus, spleen, lymph nodes, bone marrow, and antibodies.

malignant Harmful to life; specifically, in the case of a tumor, tending to metastasize.

metastasis Movement of cancer from original site in the body to secondary sites.

oncogene A gene having the potential to cause a normal cell to become cancerous.

oncologist A doctor who specializes in the diagnosis and treatment of tumors.

radiologist A doctor who specializes in the use of radiation for diagnosis and treatment.

remission A lessening of symptoms.

risk factor A hazard or danger that increases the likelihood that a person will develop cancer.

side effect The action or effect of a drug other than that which is desired. The term usually refers to negative or undesirable effects, such as a headache or nausea.

symptom Evidence of disease or abnormality in the body.

tumor An abnormal (benign or malignant) mass of tissue that arises without an obvious cause and has no function.

Where to Go for Help

In the United States

American Cancer Society
National Headquarters
1599 Clifton Road NE
Atlanta, GA 30329-4251
(800) 227-2345

American Self-Help Clearinghouse
Northwest Covenant Medical Center
25 Pocono Road
Denville, NJ 07834
(973) 625-9565

Cancer Care, Inc.
1180 Avenue of the Americas
New York, NY 10036
(212) 221-3300

Cancer Information Service (CIS)
1-800-4-CANCER

National Coalition for Cancer Survivorship (NCCS)
1010 Wayne Avenue, Fifth Floor
Silver Spring, MD 20910
(301) 650-8868

The Wellness Community
2716 Ocean Park Boulevard, Suite 1040
Santa Monica, CA 90405
(310) 314-2555

In Canada

Canadian Cancer Society
10 Alcorn Avenue, Suite 200
Toronto, Ontario
M4V 3B1
(416) 961-7223

Web Sites

American Cancer Society
http://www.cancer.org

Canadian Cancer Society
http://www.cancer.ca

CancerNet
http://www.ncc.go.jp

Cancer Survivors Online
http://www.ahamade.com/CancerSurvivors

For Further Reading

Bognar, David. *Cancer: Increasing Your Odds for Survival.* Alameda, CA: Hunter House Publishers, 1998.

Boik, John. *Cancer and Natural Medicine: A Textbook of Basic Science and Clinical Research.* Portland, OR: Oregon Medical Press, 1995.

Buckman, Robert, M.D. *What You Really Need to Know About Cancer: A Comprehensive Guide for Patients and Their Families.* Baltimore, MD: Johns Hopkins, 1995.

Cotter, Kelly Maury. *Kids with Courage: Thoughts and Stories About Growing Up with Cancer.* Madison, WI: University of Wisconsin, 1998.

Fine, Judylaine. *Afraid to Ask: A Book for Families to Share About Cancer.* New York: William Morrow, 1986.

Landau, Elaine. *Breast Cancer*. Danbury, CT: Franklin
   Watts, 1995.
Miskovitz, Paul, M.D. *What to Do If You Get Colon
   Cancer*. New York: John Wiley and Sons, 1997.
Swirsky, Joan. *The Breast Cancer Handbook*. New
   York: Harper, 1994.
Wainrib, Barbara Rubin. *Prostate Cancer: A Guide for
   Women and the Men They Love*. New York:
   Bantam, 1996.
Wallner, Kent, M.D. *Prostate Cancer: A Non-Surgical
   Perspective*. Canaan, NY: SmartMedicine Press,
   1996.

Index

About the Author

Francesca Massari is a writer and editor in California, where she also studying screenwriting.

Photo Credits

Cover and pp. 2 and 21 © Custom Medical; pp. 6, 26, 35, 36, 40, 54 by Kristen Artz; pp.10, 28, 46 © Super Stock; p. 18 © Uniphoto; p. 24 © Index Stock; p.32 by Ira Fox.

Series Design
Annie O'Donnell

Layout
Michael J. Caroleo